Fluff

A Comedy

John Scholes

Samuel French – London
New York – Sydney – Toronto – Hollywood

ESSEX COUNTY LIBRARY

CHARACTERS

Joe Goodwin
Sally Goodwin, his sister
Nigel Parkington-Lustworthy
Alice Fairweather, his girlfriend

The action takes place in a bedroom in Grinleigh Mansion, a country estate, late one night

Time — the present

FLUFF

A bedroom on the first floor of Grinleigh Mansion. The time is ten thirty at night

The room is lit only by moonlight coming through the large french windows which lead on to a balcony. The central item of furniture is a large double bed which is situated close to the french windows. Piled on the bed are several fur coats. There is a wardrobe, a dressing table and a bedside cabinet. There is a door which leads on to the corridor R. The room suggests genteel wealth and taste

As the CURTAIN *rises the room is empty. Slightly muffled noises of a party drift up from downstairs*

Joe's cockney voice is heard coming from the direction of the garden below the balcony

Joe (*off; whispering urgently*) Sally . . . Sally . . . For Gawd's sake, Sally. Are you there? (*He suddenly lets out a strangled cry of pain. Then, more urgently*) Sally . . . It's me, Joe . . . I suppose you realize it's about thirty below zero out here . . . Sally . . .

A beam of light from Joe's torch shines through the window into the room. Joe stifles another cry of pain. The light wavers up and down. Joe enters the room, gingerly rubbing his groin. He is dressed in dark sweater, trousers and plimsolls. He immediately bangs his knee on the end of the bed. Stifling another cry of pain, he rubs his knee

(*Whispering softly*) Sally . . . (*He shines his torch on the fur coats and whistles softly. Shining the torch round the room he sees the light switch beside the door. Going to it he switches on the main light. He puts the torch in his pocket, goes to the bed and picks up a fur coat which he fondles lovingly*) Cor . . . Benidorm, here we come.

The door handle clicks and the door opens slowly. The noise of the party comes through louder. Joe hastily throws down the fur coat and dives under the bed

Sally Goodwin enters cautiously, peering both ways up the corridor outside before coming into the room. She is young, attractive and is wearing a party dress. She carries a drink in her hand

Sally crosses to the window and speaks through it with a Cockney accent

Sally Joe ... Are you there, Joe? ... It's me, Sally ... Joe ...

Joe emerges from under the bed and stands behind the unsuspecting Sally

Joe ... if you're out there stop messing about ... I'm catching my death of cold standing here ...

Joe (*grimly*) And I joined the brass monkey club ten minutes ago.

Sally wheels around startled. She sighs with relief

Sally Joe ... what are you doing in here?

Joe (*pointing to the fur coats*) More importantly, what's the fluff still doing in here?

Sally (*looking at the coats*) They look like they're mating. Do you suppose they'll let us have first choice of the litter?

Joe (*unamused*) Very droll. .... It is a great comfort to me knowing that my darling sister can extract a certain amount of light-hearted frippery out of the situation.

Sally (*amused*) Light-hearted what?

Joe Frippery. .... Frippery.

Sally I've never fripped in my life.

Joe (*suspiciously*) How much have you had to drink?

Sally (*giggly*) Oh ... about a fripperful.

Joe (*stoney-faced*) You have broken the first golden, absolutely essential rule.

Sally You mean "Thou must not get thyself stoned whilst pulling a job"?

Joe Exactly. What would Mum and Dad —

Sally God rest their souls.

Joe God rest their souls — what would Mum and Dad say if they were here now?

Sally (*thinking hard*) Well ... Mum would say "Have a good time, love, while you're still young." And Dad would say "Don't take any bleeding notice of that poncey brother of yours."

Joe (*aghast*) Sally . . . they'd be disgusted with you. I set this job up with precise detail.

Sally (*sighing*) Yes, Joe, you're the eighth wonder of the criminal world.

Joe You can be sarcastic — but who was it got himself a job as a handyman for a couple of weeks in this little country estate so I could case the joint?

Sally (*having heard all this before*) You did, Einstein.

Joe And who found out there'd be a shindig on tonight for all the aristos within tally-ho distance?

Sally You did, boy wonder.

Joe And who wangled you an invite to the party as a big knob guest?

Sally (*sweetly*) You did, big brother — and thank you. I'm having an absolutely gorgeous time. (*She sips her drink*)

Joe (*exploding*) You're not supposed to be having a gorgeous time. You're supposed to be throwing certain items of clothing from that balcony. (*He grabs her drink and puts it on the bedside cabinet*)

Sally Pardon?

Joe (*with exasperation, pointing to the coats*) The fluff. The whole point of the exercise. Remember?

Sally All right, all right — keep your fluff on.

Joe Don't you realize . . .

Sally What are we arguing for?

Joe We're arguing because you were supposed to have been here ten minutes ago. Gawd, Sally, we even synchronized watches.

Sally (*moving to* R) Well, I've been having trouble with a fruitcake.

Joe I'd say the vodka and tonics have given you the most trouble.

Sally This posh toff has been giving me the lecherous bit ever since I got here. He won't leave me alone.

Joe You can handle that sort.

Sally He says I'm the most ravishing creature at the party.

Joe Well, you *did* say he was a fruitcake. Right — now I'll get back down (*rubbing his groin*) . . . and hope I don't do myself another mischief on that railing thing.

Sally Balustrades.

Joe All right, don't believe me. (*He moves to the window*)

Sally That's what they call that railing thing.

Joe Thanks to you I'm practically falsetto. Now — back to plan

A—and let's make it snappy before somebody comes in. (*He looks through the window*) Gawd, it's cold out there. (*He turns to Sally; entreating*) Please, don't take too long about it. (*He goes out on to the balcony*)

Sally (*half to herself*) He says I've got a sweet disposition.

Joe comes back into the room

Joe (*impatiently*) Who?

Sally Nigel.

Joe Nigel?

Sally Nigel Parkington-Lustworthy.

Joe (*agape*) Nigel Par . . . . You've got to be joking.

Sally (*rounding fiercely*) I *have* got a bleeding sweet disposition.

Joe (*backing off*) Of course you have, bumpkins.

Sally And don't call me bumpkins—you know I hate it.

Joe Look, just do the job you came here to do and then little sweet can get back to her fruitcake. (*He smiles at his inept joke and goes back on to the balcony*)

Sally (*going towards the door*) I'm going back to him now.

Joe comes back into the room

Joe (*greatly concerned*) What did you say?

Sally (*with her hand on the doorknob*) I'm going to enjoy myself.

Joe dashes to her and winces as he bumps his knee on the bed. He takes Sally's arm and leads her away from the door.

Joe (*pleading*) Come on now, Sal, has big, bad brother Joe upset you?

Sally (*sitting on the bed*) Yes.

Joe I'm sorry. It's just that . . . well, I was out there in the cold having my balustrades frozen, I had to climb up here—you know I haven't got a head for heights—then I find you—not here, then you turn up zonked—

Sally Half-zonked.

Joe (*with an encouraging smile*) So . . . off we go then, eh? (*He claps his hands*) Throw the fluff down to me before somebody notices my van out there and gets slightly suspicious. (*He leaps over the bed and goes out on to the balcony. He pokes his head back into the room*) All right?

Sally (*rising wearily*) All right.

Joe (*smiling*) Good girl, bump — er . . . sweetie. Give me one minute from (*he looks at his watch*) — synchronize watches.

Sally heaves a sigh of resignation and checks her watch

One minute from now. (*He hurries on to the balcony. He lets out a cry of pain as he encounters the balustrade again*)

Sally picks up a fur coat and goes towards the window

The door opens slowly and Nigel Parkington-Lustworthy enters, unseen by Sally. He is fortyish, smartly dressed, and carries a bottle of whisky. He is obviously drunk and smiles inanely as he weaves unsteadily up to Sally's back

Nigel (*in an exaggerated "posh" voice*) Found you, you little minx you.

Sally spins round. She is obviously flustered

Sally (*affecting a "posh" accent*) Oh, Nigel . . . er . . . you found me.
Nigel In the tenth bedroom I've tried . . . or is it the fiftieth? What are you up to?
Sally (*her mind racing*) Er . . . I came in here to . . . er . . .
Nigel (*lecherously*) You came to have an assignation with me, didn't you?

Nigel attempts to put his arm around Sally. She squirms out of his reach and crosses R

Sally N—no . . . I . . . (*she realizes she is holding a fur coat*) I came to put my fur coat on.
Nigel What on earth for?
Sally (*lapsing into cockney*) 'Cos I've joined the brass monkey club.
Nigel (*taken aback*) I beg your pardon?
Sally (*recovering her "posh" voice*) I was finding it a trifle piccadilly. (*She puts the fur coat on. It is far too large for her, the sleeves extending well past her fingertips*
Nigel (*crossing to Sally*) You look absolutely stunning.
Sally (*smiling sweetly*) Thanks.
Nigel (*holding up the bottle*) Here, this will warm you up for old Nigel.
Sally (*backing away*) What makes you think I want to be warmed up for you?

Nigel Oh, come now—you planned this, didn't you? You little vixen you.

Sally (*appalled*) Certainly not. I've told you—

Nigel (*with persistence*) Well, anyway, let's make the most of being alone, eh? Drinky? (*He holds up the bottle*)

Sally (*looking around*) I've got a drink somewhere. There it is.

Sally crosses L *to the bedside cabinet and picks up her drink. Nigel follows her*

Nigel (*offering the bottle*) A little top-up?

Sally (*putting her hand over the glass*) No thanks. This is vodka and tonic.

Nigel gets very close to Sally

Nigel (*intimately*) You know, you really are a spiffing little piece of work.

Sally (*coyly*) Oh, Nigel, you'll turn my head saying things like that.

Nigel (*putting his arm round her*) I'd like to turn more than your head.

Sally (*taking his arm away*) But didn't I see you come to the party with another girl?

Nigel (*unperturbed*) Alice? Oh yes, you probably did.

Sally Well then—

Nigel Alice doesn't mean a thing to me. But you . . . well, you're . . .

Sally A spiffing little piece of work?

Nigel (*putting his arm round her*) Precisely.

Sally What if she came looking for you?

Nigel No chance of that.

Sally How can you be sure?

Nigel (*gently leading Sally towards the bed*) Because she's probably with Bobby in bedroom twelve right now.

Sally Charming.

Nigel Can't you see I'm madly in love with you, you little kitten you?

Sally I'm enormously flattered but—

Nigel (*warming to his task*) Can't you see you've aroused something in me?

Sally (*becoming concerned at the situation*) Not from this angle, no.

Sally finds herself against the bed. Nigel gently pushes her on the bed and lies on top of her

Nigel Don't fight it ... er ... Lavinia ...

Sally It's Sally, actually.

Nigel (*panting slightly*) Sally, Lavinia, Arthur—what does it matter? You are you, I am I and tonight's the night.

Sally Oooh ... you do go on.

Nigel (*pressing close to her*) You must feel it.

Sally I can feel something.

Nigel (*encouraged*) Something magical?

Sally Not exactly.

Nigel Something profound?

Sally I don't think so.

Nigel Whatever it is I feel it too.

Sally Do you?

Nigel (*trying to kiss her*) Oh yes, yes, yes ...

Sally Well, why don't you get rid of it?

Nigel Why?

Sally Because it's damned hard and uncomfortable.

Sally takes out the bottle from between them. Nigel takes the bottle impatiently and puts it on the bedside cabinet L. Sally takes the opportunity to rise and sit on the edge of the bed R. Nigel climbs over the bed and sits beside her to resume his amorous advances

Nigel (*trying to slip the fur coat from Sally's shoulders*) Now, why don't we relax and—

A cry of pain from Joe, off, is suddenly heard

Sally (*trying to occupy Nigel's mind*) Yes? You were saying?

Nigel (*listening*) What was that?

Sally Chivas Regal, I think.

Nigel Not the bottle. ... I thought I heard a noise.

Sally (*nervously*) Well, there *is* a party going on.

Nigel (*looking around*) I thought I heard someone cry out.

Sally Probably Alice in the next room.

Nigel No, it was a man.

Sally Probably Bobby.

Nigel It sounded as though he was in pain.

Sally Alice must be quite a girl.

Nigel rises and goes towards the window

Nigel I could have sworn it came from—

Nigel makes a move towards the window. Sally grabs his arm and pulls him back on to the bed beside her

Sally You were telling me downstairs about your lovely country estate.
Nigel Was I?

Unseen by Sally and Nigel, Joe enters through the french windows. He rubs his groin. His face registers extreme anger as he watches the other two

Sally Yes. Tell me more about it.
Nigel (*putting his arm around her*) Would you like me to show it to you?

Joe reacts as he gets the wrong impression of the conversation

Sally I'd love you to.
Nigel It's pretty big.
Sally (*enthusiastically*) How big?
Nigel Well ... I find it takes quite a lot of handling.
Sally But you manage?
Nigel With a little bit of help.
Sally You're very lucky.
Nigel What about yours?
Sally (*slightly taken aback*) Mine?
Nigel Bobby tells me you've got quite a nice little endowment ...
Sally Oh yes ... I'm very well set up.
Nigel It must give you a good deal of pleasure ... not to mention a considerable income.
Sally (*with a show of modesty*) Well, I'm thinking of opening it to the public.
Nigel I hope that doesn't mean I'll have to pay to see it.
Sally Oh no, but I'd like to see yours first.

Joe is appalled. Having heard enough, he picks up the bottle from the bedside cabinet and goes behind Nigel. He raises the bottle to strike Nigel on the back of the head. Sally looks up as the bottle is about to descend, and she lets out an involuntary half scream. Nigel rises suddenly. Joe dashes back to the balcony, taking the bottle with him

Nigel (*alarmed*) What's up?
Sally (*with wide-eyed innocence*) Er ... up?

Nigel You screamed.

Sally Me? I never do things like that.

Nigel But—

Sally (*pulling the fur coat around her*) I'm just a bit cold, that's all. I've got the shivers.

Nigel (*crossing to the window*) No wonder you're cold. (*He closes the window and puts the catch on*)

Sally (*rising*) I really think we should get back to the party.

Nigel (*crossing to Sally*) Nonsense. We're having our party here. (*He has his back to the window*)

Joe appears at the window and grimaces and gesticulates angrily at Sally who can see him as she faces Nigel)

Sally (*going towards Nigel and putting her arms tenderly around his neck*) But we can come back here later. (*Over Nigel's shoulder she motions vigorously to Joe to get out of sight*)

Nigel (*pleased at her apparent surrender*) What? And find some other couple have taken over our little love nest? No fear.

Sally (*furiously signalling to Joe*) But there are lots of other bedrooms.

Nigel Nearly all occupied. You'd be amazed at some of the sights I've barged in on while I was searching for you. (*Pondering*) I never realized that Rodney had a thing for Fiona.

Joe continues to signal to Sally to get rid of Nigel. Sally signals "How?"

Sally Why don't you get a bottle of drink?

Nigel (*breaking from Sally*) No need, old bean, we've got a plentiful supply. (*He goes to the bedside cabinet to get the bottle and does a double-take when he realizes it is not there*)

Sally What's the matter?

Nigel I could have sworn . . . (*He looks under the bed and round the floor and then goes towards the window*)

Joe ducks out of sight as Nigel approaches

Sally (*drawing Nigel away from the window*) Please, darling, be a sweetie and go and get some refreshments.

Nigel But I could have sworn . . .

Sally (*putting her arms around his neck; seductively*) Please, Nigel. I'll keep any intruders at bay.

Nigel (*overwhelmed*) Oh, I say.

Sally (*husky with emotion*) And then ... you and I can ... well ...
we can ...

Nigel I say, you really are a bit of all right, aren't you?

Sally (*pouting*) Take your time. I want to be ... prepared.

Nigel (*wilting*) Oh, gosh ...

Sally pushes Nigel towards the door

Sally (*opening the door*) Anybody ever tell you you've got a sexy
smile?

Nigel (*smiling sexily*) Well ... I ... as a matter of fact—

*Sally pushes Nigel through the door and closes it. She waits for a
moment to see if he will come back. She then hurries to the window,
releases the catch and opens it. Joe enters shivering and angry*

Joe I can't leave you out of my sight for a minute. Even a bleedin'
synchronized minute.

Sally is on the defensive and resumes her Cockney accent

Sally Don't huff and puff at me.

Joe Don't huff and—? Listen, Miss Hot-Pants, have you forgotten
the purpose of our presence here?

Sally (*angrily*) No, I have not.

Joe Then, if you could possibly get your mind off the other and
concentrate it on the job I'd be very grateful.

Sally You're disgusting.

Joe (*amazed*) *I'm* disgusting? After hearing you and Lord Faunt-
leroy I think you've got a nerve. All that "I'll show you mine if
you show me yours." You're perverted.

Sally Will you leave off. I'm doing my best.

Joe I can see that.

Sally (*emphatically*) I've done my last job with you.

Joe You've broken the second most golden rule. Never get
romantically inclined on a job.

Sally Did you hear me?

Joe Mum and Dad would be very disappointed in you, Sal. God
rest their souls.

Sally I said—did you hear me?

Joe Sure I did. You've said that before. Now, let's get these furs

where they belong. I'll go down below — synchronize watches —
and then you —

Sally I'm not doing it.

Joe (*ignoring her*) And then you drop the fluff down to me.

Sally (*with determination*) I said — I'm not doing it.

Joe 'Course you are, Sal. D'you realize how much all this lot's
worth?

Sally A holiday in Benidorm.

Joe Right.

Sally I'm not doing it.

Joe Look, Sal, I'm sorry if I said anything out of place —

Sally I can have a lot more than a measly holiday in Benidorm.

Joe There'll be a lot left over for other things. You can have that
pressure cooker you've always dreamed about.

Sally I could also have a country estate, a grouse moor, servants —
and holidays in the Bahamas.

Joe (*non-plussed*) You think this upper class twit's going to marry
you?

Sally If I play my cards right.

Joe Oh come on, Sal, we've had this sort of thing before.
Remember how you envied Barney Cohen's missus because he
bought her a big, red Volvo?

Sally Barney's a big operator.

Joe (*hurt*) Aren't I? (*He picks up a fur coat*) Look at this lot — just
waiting to be nicked. You'll have a big, red Volvo, if that's what
you want.

Sally I want respectability.

Joe (*sighing*) Oh, not that again.

Sally Yes — that again.

Joe Well, you pick your moments, don't you?

Sally I'm sorry, Joe, I'm just not cut out for this sort of work.

Joe (*looking heavenwards*) She didn't mean it, Mum and Dad. It's
just a momentary abomination.

Sally Anyway, you don't need me.

Joe 'Course I need you. We're a team.

Sally You've been up and down that drainpipe like a sewer rat —
why can't you just grab the furs yourself? It'd save a lot of time
and arguing.

Joe I've told you — we do everything together.

Sally (*crossing to the door*) Well, I'm going to marry a rich landowner—see if *that's* something we can do together.

Joe (*sitting on the bed; dejectedly*) All right, bumpkins. Split up the family act. Be selfish.

Sally (*opening the door*) I'm not being selfish—and don't call me bumpkins.

Joe (*utterly woebegone*) You've broken the third golden rule—never desert your confederate in his hour of greatest need.

Sally (*closing the door; relenting slightly*) Oh, Joe, leave off. Take the flaming furs—they're all yours.

Joe (*looking heavenwards*) It's not my fault, Mum and Dad. I'm as stunned as you must be. Try to forgive her.

Sally (*crossing to Joe*) Joe . . .

Joe (*heavenward*) It's not as though this chinless ponce has even proposed to her.

Sally He will.

Joe (*heavenward*) Haven't I looked after her? Haven't I treated her right? Where did I go wrong? (*He buries his head in his hands*)

Sally Oh, for. . . . Get down below. I'll chuck the damned fluff to you.

Joe springs enthusiastically to his feet and smiles

Joe (*looking at his watch*) Give me a minute. Now, synchronize—

Sally (*impatiently*) Yes, yes I know. (*She looks at her watch*) One minute from—now.

Joe vaults over the bed and exits through the french window, climbing down from the balcony

Joe (*calling off*) You're a great kid, Sal.

Sally Yeah, yeah, I know. I'm all heart. Watch out for the . . .

Joe, off, gives a cry of pain

. . . balustrade.

Sally takes off the coat she is wearing and goes on to the balcony. She throws the coat down to Joe

(*Calling*) Here, Joe, put this on. It'll help keep out the cold. (*She goes to the bed and picks up a fur coat. She looks at her watch and waits. Then she goes to the french window with the coat*)

There is a knock at the door. Sally freezes

The door opens and Alice Fairweather enters. She is attractive and is wearing a party dress

Alice looks round the room and is startled to see Sally. When she speaks it is at first with a well-to-do accent, but she later lapses into a North-Country accent

Alice Oh, hello ... I didn't think there was anyone here.

Sally (*reverting to a "posh" accent*) Oh yes ... there's just little me.

Alice I'm ... er ... I'm not feeling too well. A little tiddly, I'm afraid.

Sally Oh dear. Perhaps you should go home.

Alice What? And miss all the fun?

Sally Not much fun being sick all over the place.

Alice (*going to the bed*) I thought I'd have a little lie down.

Sally (*slightly perturbed*) Here?

Alice (*sweetly*) You don't mind, do you?

Sally (*flustered*) Well, I ... no, not at all.

Alice (*sitting on the bed*) Thanks. Rather over indulged, I'm afraid.

Sally goes to Alice and puts a fur coat on Alice's shoulders

Sally That'll keep you warm at least.

Alice Thank you.

Sally puts the pillow against the head of the bed

Sally Here, you lie back on that and put your feet up.

Alice (*obeying instructions*) I feel such a silly ninny. (*She looks closely at Sally*) Aren't you the girl ... er ... Nigel's been pursuing all evening?

Sally Yes. You're Alice, aren't you?

Alice Yes. You don't happen to know where the dear boy is, do you?

Sally Not exactly.

Alice I don't suppose you could find him for me? Tell him his little flower has wilted somewhat?

Sally (*glancing nervously at the window*) Well ... it's a little bit awkward ...

Alice (*cheerfully*) It's all right. Actually, my handbag is in here somewhere. I've got something in it I can take.

Sally (*looking around*) What's it look like?

Alice Red with white trimmings. (*She points to the wardrobe*) I think it's in there.

Sally crosses to the wardrobe. She opens it and looks inside

Sally (*half inside the wardrobe*) Red, did you say?

Alice Yes. Can't you find it?

Sally goes inside the wardrobe. With great speed, Alice leaps to the wardrobe. She slams it shut and turns the key in the lock

Sally (*banging on the wardrobe*) Hey, what's going on?

Alice (*feigning concern*) Oh dear, the door appears to have slammed shut. I can't open it—it seems to be jammed. Just hang on a tick and I'll go and see if I can find anyone to let you out. Don't worry.

The knocking from inside the wardrobe ceases. Alice tiptoes to the window

Alice (*calling softly through window, with a North-Country accent*) Badger? . . . Badger, are you there? . . . Badger . . .

Unseen by Alice the door opens and Nigel enters carrying a bottle of vodka. He sees Alice and, thinking it is Sally, creeps up behind her. He puts his arms around her tightly

Nigel (*triumphantly*) Got you, you little tadpole you.

Alice spins around and faces Nigel. His smile freezes

Alice (*angrily*) Badger!

Nigel (*slipping into a North-Country accent*) Alice! (*Looking around*) Where's—

Alice That little upper crust tart you've been chasing ever since we got here?

Nigel Just a bit of fun.

Alice Fun? Don't give me that. You're always the same. Play a part for five minutes and you get to thinking you're Robert Morley in the Barretts of Wapping Street.

Nigel Can't I just have a bit of fun?

Alice I know you, Badger Brockwell. You think you can get some unsuspecting wealthy heiress to marry you one day and then it's "You've had yours, Alice—thank you and goodbye."

Nigel Can't see why I can't have a bit of fun.

Alice We're on a job. Fun later—if at all.

Nigel You don't like me having fun.

Alice Oh shut up. Now get down under that balcony where you're supposed to be and get ready to collect the furs as I throw them out.

Nigel I'm not climbing down there.

Alice (*speaking as if to a child*) Go downstairs, out the back way, make your way round to here and make sure nobody sees you. I'll give you five minutes.

Nigel puts the vodka bottle on the bedside cabinet

Nigel (*looking at his watch*) Synchronize watches?

Alice (*pushing him to the door*) Oh for heaven's sake, get going. (*She opens the door*)

Nigel You never have any fun.

Alice pushes Nigel through the door. She closes it and heaves a sigh of relief. A sudden cry of pain comes from the balcony. She becomes alarmed and looks for somewhere to hide

Joe (*off, calling softly*) Sally ... remember me? Your partner ... Sally ...

Alice goes to the wardrobe but remembers that Sally is in there. She stops, looks around, and settles for under the bed

Joe enters from the balcony holding his groin. He is wearing the fur coat that Sally threw from the balcony. He looks around the room

All right, Sally. What's the name of this game? Freeze the pants off brother Joe? (*He goes to look under the bed but is stopped by banging from the wardrobe. He crosses to the wardrobe*) That you, Sal?

Sally No, it's Eamonn Andrews and *This is Your Life*.

Joe unlocks the wardrobe and Sally emerges

Joe The things you'll do to get out of helping me. We came to rob the place not haunt it.

Sally (*looking around*) She's gone.

Joe Who?

Sally (*seething*) So she thinks she can keep me away from her boyfriend that way, the jealous hussy.

Joe Who?

Sally I'll show her. It's no holds barred now. I heard her talking to some bloke or other.

Joe Who?

Sally It sounded like George Formby. I couldn't make out what they were saying though.

Joe For Gawd's sake, who?

Sally I'll find him — and if my name isn't Sally Parkington-Lustworthy before long I'm not Sally Goodwin.

Sally marches to the door and exits

Joe stands bewildered and helpless. After a short pause to collect himself he goes to the bed and picks up a fur coat. A wistful look comes into his eye. Suddenly he becomes determined

Joe Right, my girl. All mine, are they? Right. You'll be sorry. (*Looking heavenward*) You heard what she said. "They're all yours" she said. (*He picks up an armful of coats, goes to the window and peers out to see if the coast is clear*)

The door opens and Nigel puts his head cautiously round

Joe does not see Nigel, and goes on to the balcony

Nigel Some silly sod's got his van parked outside. I ... (*He breaks off as he sees the room is empty*)

Nigel enters the room

Seeing Joe on the balcony in the fur coat Nigel thinks it is Sally. He creeps up to the window and waits in ambush. Joe comes back into the room to collect the rest of the coats. Nigel pounces and puts his arms round Joe's waist

Nigel (*in his posh voice*) Got you again, you little shrew, you.

Joe, startled, releases Nigel's grip with a neat judo flick then faces Nigel in an aggressive karate pose. Nigel backs away in surprise

Joe You must be Nigel Parkington-whatsit.

Nigel (*confused*) Bedworthy — no, that's not right ...

Joe (*offering his hand*) Pleased to meet you.

Nigel Oh, jolly good show.

Nigel reaches for Joe's hand. Joe suddenly pulls him off balance and throws him on the bed. He pounces on Nigel and puts his hands to the latter's throat

Joe (*shaking Nigel violently*) Do you know the trouble you've caused me, eh?

Nigel (*choking*) I say, steady on—

Joe You've given me the runaround long enough.

Nigel (*gasping*) I can't recall that I've had the pleasure—

Joe loosens his grip. He looks around and sees the vodka bottle on the bedside cabinet. He picks it up and raises it threateningly

Joe I ought to bounce this off your poncey bonce.

Nigel looks more closely at Joe and suddenly realizes he has met him before. He reverts to his North-Country accent

Nigel Yes I have!

Joe (*puzzled*) You have what?

Nigel (*smiling*) Had the pleasure.

Joe Not with me, you haven't. (*He threatens with the bottle*) 'Ere, what are you insinuating, eh?

Nigel Joe Goodwin? Right?

Joe, surprised, relaxes his hostile attitude and lowers the arm holding the bottle

Joe (*warily*) I might be.

Nigel Badger. Badger Brockwell. Wormwood Scrubs. Petty larceny. Six months with good behaviour.

Joe Well—strike me. Badger.

Nigel Small world, eh?

Joe What's with the Derek Nimmo bit?

Nigel Look, er—d'you think we could discuss this vertical? Somebody might come in and get the wrong impression.

Joe removes himself from Nigel and replaces the bottle on the bedside cabinet. Nigel rises and crosses R as he adjusts his clothing and hair

Joe (*picking up a fur coat and looking hard at Nigel's back*) 'Ere, I know what a little tealeaf like you is doing here.

Nigel (*turning to Joe*) Well, I'm here to pinch the furs.

Joe No kidding?

Nigel (*confidentially*) But I've got this smashing little rich bird just eating out of my hand.

Joe That a fact?

Nigel She's worth a mint.

Joe And you're going to get your sticky little fingers on it, I suppose?

Nigel (*gleefully rubbing his hands*) Am I ever. She's just nice and ripe to fall for the old Brockwell charm.

Joe And what about the fluff?

Nigel Yes, you're right. First things first. (*He picks up the coats and goes to the window*)

Joe There's already some on the balcony.

Nigel Oh?

Nigel puts the coats back on the bed and goes through the window to the balcony. Joe picks up the vodka bottle, kisses it meaningfully, and grimly follows Nigel. There is a muffled thud, followed by a grunt and groan from Nigel. Joe comes back into the room, dragging Nigel's inert form

Joe We may have done porridge together, Badger old son, but this is no time for sentiment.

Joe puts Nigel on the bed. The door opens suddenly and Joe ducks behind the edge of the bed, peering over to see what is happening

   Sally enters

She comes into the room, closes the door, and goes to the bed. Joe rises and faces her

Sally (*seeing Nigel's prostrate form*) What are you doing with him?

Joe He's flaked out. He's been hitting the bottle too much.

Sally kneels on the bed beside Nigel and tries to revive him

Sally I think he's coming round.

Joe Sal, will you forget about him? Believe me, he's not worth it.

Sally Oh buzz off, Joe—and take your precious furs with you.

Joe Sal, let me tell you about him. He's—

Sally suddenly sits up listening intently

Sally Shush! I think somebody's coming.

Joe heads for the window

   No—not out there. It's too cold. Get under the bed.

Sally is intent on reviving Nigel as Joe dashes to R of the bed. He lifts the counterpane and stoops to get under the bed. As he gets down a leg belonging to Alice appears and kicks him furiously away. Sally does not see this. Joe straightens up and does a double-take. Bemused, he gets into the wardrobe

Are you all right under there, Joe?

Alice gives a low, masculine grunt of assertion. Sally smiles wickedly and starts to speak loudly to Nigel's unconscious form for Joe's benefit

Oh, Nigel, you've come round. Are you all right? (*She giggles*) Ooh ... you are feeling fresh, aren't you? (*She giggles*)

Nigel continues to snore gently

Nigel! What are you doing? (*She makes exaggerated kissing noises*) Yes, darling, and I love you, too. Would you really? You say the sweetest things ... I have a confession to make, dearheart — I'm not really wealthy and I don't own a big estate ... I knew you'd say that ... what's that? You still want to marry me? Oh, darling, you're wonderful. ... Of course I accept. (*She makes kissing noises*) ... Oh, Nigel, you're so strong and virile. ... Oh ... Oh dear me ... Oh ... Oh ... (*She jumps up and down on the bed*) ... Oh, can I have a big red Volvo? ... Oh, Nigel, thank you. ... (*She gets carried away by false passion as she jumps up and down*) ... Oh, you're a marvellous lover. ... Oh ... (*Completely immersed in her act she stands on the bed and makes kissing and moaning noises as she jumps wildly up and down*)

Joe, then Alice, poke their heads from their hiding places and watch Sally, fascinated. Then Nigel wakes up and he too watches Sally's actions with a bemused stare as he rubs the back of his head

Oh, I just know we're going to be happy together ... (*Sally stops her performance as she realizes Nigel is awake*)

Joe and Alice withdraw to their hiding places

(*To Nigel, loudly*) Yes, darling, I think you are right. We should join the party.

Sally pushes Nigel off the bed. He picks himself up, still groggy and unsure of what is happening. Sally pushes him forcefully towards the door. Nigel obeys without dissent. Sally takes Nigel's arm

(Loudly in the direction of the bed) You can tell me more about your grouse moor and I'll tell you about my grotty brother.

Sally opens the door and she and Nigel exit

Joe emerges from the wardrobe. His face registers amazement. He crosses to the bed and peers under

Joe I don't think we've been formally introduced.

Alice's hand comes out from under the bed. Joe shakes it

Alice Alice Fairweather.
Joe Joe Goodwin.
Alice Waddya know, Joe?
Joe I'd like to know if there's any more to you than an arm and a leg—lovely though both may be.

Alice emerges from under the bed

Alice That was my boyfriend your sister just waltzed off with.
Joe Badger?
Alice Yes.
Joe *(smiling)* She thinks he's loaded with grouse moors.
Alice The only grousing he's ever done is after he's bet on a fast-finishing second at Newmarket.
Joe *(grinning)* And he thinks she's got a big endowment.
Alice *(smiling widely)* I know.
Joe The only thing she's endowed with is for sitting on.

They both laugh uproariously

Alice *(seriously)* Right. Now you get down below.
Joe Right you are. *(He crosses to the window)*
Alice *(picking up the furs)* I'll give you a minute.
Joe *(looking at his watch)* Synchronize watches.
Alice *(impatiently)* Oh, get going. And watch out for the bal—

Joe's exit is followed by a long drawn-out howl as he falls from the balcony to the ground below. There is a loud crash

Alice sighs, shakes her head and takes the furs out on to the balcony

CURTAIN

FURNITURE AND PROPERTY LIST

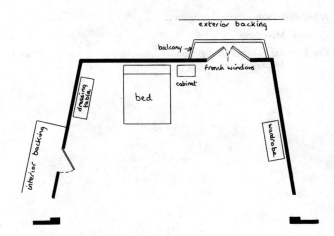

On stage: Wardrobe
Bed. *On it:* Fur coats piled haphazardly
Bedside Cabinet
Dressing Table

The stage should be dressed to suggest genteel wealth and taste

Off stage: Torch **(Joe)**
Spirits glass with vodka and tonic **(Sally)**
Bottle of Whisky **(Nigel)**
Bottle of Vodka **(Nigel)**

LIGHTING PLOT

A bedroom. Same scene throughout.

To open: Moonlight

Cue 1   Joe switches the light on   (Page 1)
           Main lights on

EFFECTS PLOT

Cue 1 **As the C** URTAIN **rises**   (Page 1)
Muffled music and party noises

Cue 2 **As Sally enters**   (Page 1)
Increase party noise, fade as door closes

Cue 3 **Nigel goes on to the balcony followed by Joe** (Page 18)
Muffled noise of Nigel falling to the floor

Cue 4 **Alice:** "... watch out for the bal ..." (Page 20)
Crashing noise of Joe falling from the balcony

MADE AND PRINTED IN GREAT BRITAIN BY
LATIMER TREND & COMPANY LTD PLYMOUTH

MADE IN ENGLAND